Float Fishing for Steelhead
Techniques & Tackle

Dave Vedder

A Frank **A**mato

PORTLAND

Dedication:

This book is dedicated to those of you who are completely consumed by steelheading. You know who you are. You can't cross a bridge, even in the dark, without craning your neck to check out the water conditions. You are willing, nay eager, to stand hip deep in freezing water, with the rain slowly dripping into your undershorts if there's even a remote chance of a hook-up. Your fiftieth "last cast" usually happens after it's too dark to see the lure land. You will drive nine hours to fish eight. There is no cure—you know that. Maybe this book will relieve the symptoms for just a little while. But I should warn you it may just make things worse.

Acknowledgments

This is my first book. It may well be my last. It could not have happened without the selfless assistance of those who know much more about steelheading than I. Those who helped the most were Nick Amato, George Frisky, Fred Helmer, Mick Thill and Doug Wilson, But it was Pam, my best friend, my lover, my wife, who made it possible.

Published in 1995 by Frank Amato Publications, Inc.
P.O. Box 82112, Portland, Oregon 97282
(503) 653-8108
ISBN: 1-51788-039-9
UPC: 0-66066-00230-3
Illustrations by Dürten Kampmann on pages 25, 29, 37, 39, 47, 48, 56
Book Design: Charlie Clifford
Printed in Hong Kong
1 3 5 7 9 10 8 6 4 2

Contents

Introduction

Chances are the first fish you ever caught was on a bobber and a worm. I know mine was. I vividly remember that first fish, a diminutive yellow perch that jiggled my red and white plastic float a half dozen times before tentatively pulling it under. When Dad whispered, "Strike," I did, for all I was worth. That tiny perch was unceremoniously yanked out of Spencer Lake and into the warm summer afternoon, where it ended up wrapped around Dad's neck. That humble beginning launched not only a small perch but a lifetime of angling adventures.

Like so many others, I soon abandoned the bobber, or float as we now call them, and progressed to spinners, flies, and other lures. Eventually, I was bitten by the steelhead bug, and bitten badly. Soon, I neglected most other fishing pursuits to focus of North America's premier sport fish, the steelhead. For years I believed that bottom bouncing and pulling plugs were the two most effective ways to take these chrome battlers. I now know better.

I had to be shown the truth several times before I gave up my stubbornly held beliefs and began exploring the possibilities offered by float fishing. I hope others, perhaps in part due to this book, will learn the lesson more quickly than me.

My first brush with float fishing for steelhead came on a five-day steelhead safari to British Columbia. Our guide on that trip was an expert steelhead float fisher. He guided our group of five anglers on a whirlwind tour, visiting the Vedder, Chehalis, Stamp, and Sprout rivers. Everyone in our group had considerable experience steelheading with traditional bottom bouncing tackle, but none had tried float fishing. We quickly noticed that B.C. steelheaders all used long rods and floats.

The first run we fished was a pool at the entrance to a canyon. A wide gravel bar provided access to the tail of the pool. The head was inaccessible, hemmed in on both sides by vertical rock walls. Steelhead were there, lots of them, but they were stacked beneath the three-foot cascade at the head of the pool. Our traditional bottom bouncing gear was useless. We could cast upstream to where the fish held, but the resultant slack line retrieves almost inevitably snagged bottom. Even when we avoided the snags, we couldn't detect the bites.

Our guide, on the other hand, had no problems with his floats. He simply flicked his float to the head of the pool and took up the slack as his float merrily bobbed back toward him. That is, until it suddenly slid beneath the surface! "There he is," he announced and quickly handed off the rod to one of his customers. As quick as that, four more bottom bouncers began their conversion to flat fishing. By the end of our trip, everyone was using float rods and perhaps, more importantly, everyone was catching steelhead on a method that was completely new to them.

My first steelhead on a float rod came on that same trip. We were fishing the Vedder River. It was high and muddy—right on the ragged edge of being unfishable. From a dike ten feet above the thundering brown water, our guide flipped his float halfway across the river to work a slick behind a bathtub-sized boulder. I was marveling at the precision of his cast and the ease with which he was working his float in the swirling current, when suddenly the float went down. Then, to my surprise, he handed me the rod.

I soon learned why they sometimes call single action reels knuckle busters. The big steelhead turned sideways and let the current sweep him nearly 150 feet downstream before tucking into the quiet water at the edge of the rip-rap dike. Slowly, I learned how to work the single action reel, palming the rim for added drag, quickly releasing the spinning handles when the fish wanted to run.

Eventually, the fish moved upstream to a position just below our feet. Quicker than I can tell the story, the big buck dashed upstream brushing the line against a jagged rock. The line held for an instant, then parted. The fish went free. I have been hooked on float fishing ever since.

I acknowledge that many others have used floats long before I discovered their pleasures, and that many other are far better steelheaders than I. It is the experience and knowledge of these experts that has made this book possible, my hope was merely to serve as the conduit through which the knowledge of these top steelheaders flows. I hope you find I have done my work well.

The author with a hatchery steelhead taken with a float and bait rig on Idaho's Clearwater River.

The Basics

In any sport the pursuit of excellence begins with an analysis of the basic aspects. In his formula for baseball success, Bill Mazeroski said,"They throw the ball, I hit it; they hit the ball, I catch it."—simplicity to the extent it seems valueless. But not so. No matter how far we want to travel on the road to excellence we must master the basics before we can progress further. For the steelheader the basics are these: You must fish where the fish are. You must present your bait or lure in a natural manner. You must know when the fish has taken the lure. All else is superfluous, if you haven't mastered these seemingly obvious basic tenants.

Why fish with floats? No other system of steelheading will as consistently put your lure where the fish are in a natural manner, while signaling the most tentative strike or pick-up. Let's look at each of these basic elements of successful steelheading and see how the float gives the steelheader the edge that lets them proceed further toward the pursuit of excellence in freshwater angling's most challenging, thus most satisfying, pursuit.

Fishing Where the Fish Are

A later chapter (see page 43) discusses the elements of reading water. For now we will look at the essentials of presenting the lure in the steelhead's strike zone, assuming we have decided where they are most likely to lie.

In almost every case, steelhead are on or near the river bottom. Sometimes they will be literally touching bottom with their bellies. A float, which is rapidly and infinitely adjustable, allows you to quickly adjust to the depth of each run you fish. Once you decide the most likely lie for a steelhead, all you must do is estimate the depth of proper presentation, slide your float an appropriate distance from the lure and make your cast.

A float gives you the ability to fish exactly where the fish hold. Here, Clint Derlago uses a float to work a fishy looking seam on China Creek.

The easiest way to drift your lure over a suspected lie is to cast the float a few feet past the desired line of drift. Then reel in until the float is exactly on the course you want. On your first cast one of two things will happen: Either your lure will reach the bottom and drag along it, or your lure will drift freely above the bottom.

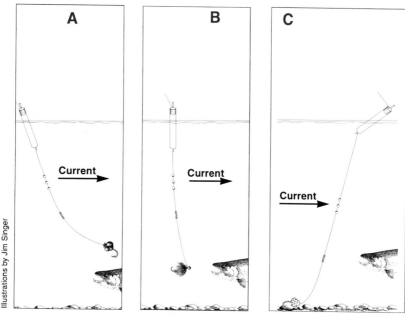

A. *Properly adjusted float. Note the float is tilted slightly upstream. This allows the angler to control the speed of the float and be ready to set the hook.*
B. *This float is properly adjusted for depth and is weighted correctly. The straight up and down attitude indicates that the lure is not touching bottom.*
C. *This float is adjusted too deep. The downstream tilt shows that the lure is dragging the bottom.*

The goal is to present your lure just above the fish. Steelhead often move higher in the water column to take a lure, they seldom move deeper to do so. A lure presented below the steelhead is of no value and may spook the fish.

If your lure is dragging bottom, the float will tilt downstream and pull underwater each time your lure snags bottom. This float behavior tells you that your lure is too deep. You will need to shorten the distance between the float and lure by a foot or so. Repeat this until the float drifts along without touching bottom or does so only rarely.

When working a run for the first time, it is best to err on the short side when adjusting the distance between the float and the lure. Unless you have seriously erred in estimating the depth of the run, you should have your lure at the right depth with only two or three adjustments. If the float signals that your lure is not hitting bottom, you may want to lengthen the distance between your float and lure until you know the depth of the run. Once you know the depth, adjust the float so that your lure drifts from six inches to two feet above the bottom.

You have now achieved the first element of successful steelheading. You are fishing where the fish are.

Presenting Your Lure Naturally

Steelhead live in a constantly moving environment. Above them air bubbles, choppy water, leaves and floating debris continuously move in a rhythm and speed dictated by the hydraulics of their river. Underwater, an array of free-floating objects ranging from salmon eggs to bits of aquatic vegetation pass by the steelhead in an endless parade. The size, shape and even color of these visual stimuli is remarkably diverse, but the one thing they all have in common is that they float naturally, in harmony with the currents of the river.

Most river fish will respond to a lure presented with a natural drift like that provided by a float. This Chinook salmon inhaled a drift bobber and Jensen Egg combo fished under a float.

When we present our lure for the steelhead's inspection, we make every effort to conceal the fact that this is an unnatural object intruding in the steelhead's environment. To that end we use long, light leaders, lines that blend with the water color and small hooks or lures. Only float fishing allows a natural presentation with our lure merrily drifting along at exactly the speed of the current while moving downstream naturally.

Natural presentation when float fishing is usually achieved by free spooling line once the float has been properly positioned in the drift. All that's needed is to push a button or thumb-bar on the reel or to move your palm away from the rim of a single action reel, and the current will do the rest. Where narrow slots speed the current, your float and lure also pick up speed. In slower drifts your float and lure slow to the speed of the steelhead's natural environment.

Seldom will a bit of yarn or roe dancing along in the water column beneath your float spook a steelhead. This is not always the case with other methods of steelheading which often result in snags that must be yanked free.

There are times when steelheaders may wish to slow the presentation of their lure. This is often the case when using spinners and jigs under a float or when working deep runs where the surface speed is considerably greater than the flow nearer the bottom. Again, this is extraordinarily simple. An educated thumb on the spool of a level-wind reel or a palm on a single action reel, allows you to walk your lure downstream at any speed you choose.

Detecting a Strike

Those who steelhead without benefit of a float, often advise newcomers that learning to detect a strike or pick-up is the key to becoming an expert steelheader. Before I was introduced to float fishing, the business of learning to tell a strike from a minor obstruction on the bottom was the most frustrating aspect of the sport. Time and again I would set the hook when nothing was there. Then, after a dozen false alarms, I would lift my rod to pull the lure free from a "hang-up" only to have my "hang-up" shake its head and spit the hook before I could get the message from my brain to my hand to set the hook! Almost all of the difficulties in detecting strikes and quickly setting the hook are eliminated by using a float.

Your float is a highly visible strike indicator. When the float goes under—Strike!

In most situations the observant angler will notice some minor jiggling or hesitation in the float's progress before the strike takes it fully under. This is a warning to get ready. For best results in hook-setting, most anglers like to wait until the float is fully underwater before striking. Once it is underwater, strike and strike hard.

Like every other aspect of steelheading, there is no hard and simple rule regarding what a strike looks like or how you should respond. Sometimes the fish pick up the lure and drift along beneath the float. When this happens, the float will pop up and float higher than before. Absolutely nothing but a fish will cause your float to pop up, when it does, strike, and strike hard.

Sometimes, the steelhead pick-up the lure and head upstream. Again nothing but a fish will make your float go upstream. That's a fish! Strike!

It can be difficult to tell the bottom from a strike. Sometimes a boulder in the middle of the run will cause your float to tip or go under. If the float tips with the bottom suddenly pointing upstream, this may be a fish that has taken the bait and remained stationary, or it may be a snag. There's no way to tell the difference, so strike and hope for the best. If it's a fish, you are in business. If it was a rock, your quick hook-set offers the best hope of eliminating a break-off.

It's hard to overdo your hook-set when fishing with long rods and making long casts. This angler demonstrates the proper technique.

If your float has drifted on a given line several times without touching bottom, the only thing that will make your float go under is a fish. It's really as simple as that. When the float goes under, Strike!

Remember that the combination of long rods, stretchy monofilament and the long distance between you and the float all tend to dampen your hook-set. Unless you are using light lines, it is almost impossible to overdo your hook-set. Bill Davis, an expert steelheader and guide, advises his clients to reel down until all slack is out of the line, then rare back as if trying to hit themselves in the seat of the pants with their rod tip. He's right on target. A solid hookset is the key to landing most of your hookups. The only way to assure a solid hook-set is with a big league strike.

There will be times when the battle begins without a solid hook-set. Often in fast moving water the moment the steelhead stops the lure, the drag caused by the current will snatch the line tight. When this happens, your first indication of a strike may be seeing the fish leap. It is still important to get a good hook-set. If you don't, odds are the fish will throw the hook before you can beach it.

Do not attempt to set the hook while the fish is jumping or taking line. Wait until you have steady pressure on the fish, then make two or three sharp, fast upward sweeps with the rod tip. Remember not to allow any slack when dropping the rod tip between hook-sets, and don't strike as hard as you can. Imagine the hook as a nail you are driving in with several sharp raps instead of one sledge hammer blow.

On occasion the hook will come free as you attempt your hook-set. This suggests that the fish was poorly hooked. Chances are you would have lost this fish in any event. You will lose far more fish by failing to set the hook than by erring in the other direction.

When everything comes together, the results can be exhilarating. This chrome April steelhead was taken on the Vedder River by Steve Carpenter.

It's true, we need to stop to look around to savor the beauty of our surroundings when we spend a day on the river. You never know who will be looking back at you.

The History of Float Fishing for Steelhead

"Let me live harmlessly, and near the brink
Of Trent or Avon and have a dwelling place;
Where I may see my quill or cork down sink
With eager bite of Perch or Bleak or Dace;
And on the world and my creator think:"
—Sir Henry Wotton, 1645

As you can see from the above quotation, anglers have used floats for hundreds of years. Angling for sport precedes the birth of Christ. In approximately 400 B.C. Plato admonished his students to take care lest they fall so passionately in love with fishing they fail to pay sufficient attention to other duties—advice many of us might do well to heed today.

In more recent times, angling became a favorite pastime of the English aristocrats. Fly fishing was a popular form of the Englishman's sport but, so too, was bait fishing. Izaak Walton in his immortal book, *The Compleat Angler,* discusses several methods of preparing baits of insects, fishes and pastes designed to draw the fish with their enticing smell. Every serious angler had a favorite paste recipe, many incorporated such strange concoctions as blood, cow dung, cheese, honey, egg-yolk and fat. Most often, these baits were suspended by a float of quill or cork.

Floats were used by the English squires of the 1800s much as they are today, both to keep the bait above bottom and to move the bait to the fish. On rivers, bladders, bottles and bundles of straw were used to transport the bait downstream. Some enterprising anglers used geese for floats. They tied their baited fishing line to the goose's leg, the goose was then chased across the waterway causing the bait to be trolled.

There were no steelheaders in old England but there were many extraordinarily dedicated river anglers. William Scrope who fished salmon during the late 1800s offered this advice to river anglers:

> Should you be of delicate temperament, and be wading in the month of February when it may chance to freeze very hard, pull down your stockings and examine your legs. Should they be, black or even purple, it might, perhaps, be as well to get on dry land; but if they are only rubicund, you may continue to enjoy the water.

The author shows off a mid-winter steelhead taken when it was so cold artisan springs froze solid the moment they hit the air. Modern steelheaders can be every bit as dedicated as our pioneer ancestors.

Had Scrope lived in modern times, he no doubt would have been a steelheader.

In an early reference to sport fishing in the Northwest, Captain John Gorgon of the HMS *America* expressed dismay that the Pacific salmon, though plentiful, failed to rise to the fly as did the salmon of his native England. Gorgon's party did catch fish but only by trolling, a practice he described as an "awful manner," to catch such mighty fish.

By the time the first settlers came west, fishing tackle had evolved to the point that it resembled today's tackle in many ways. Rods were of wood or bamboo ranging to eighteen feet in length. They were usually made with two or three sections held together by splices or brass ferrules. Reels were in common use. Some had multiplier gears, but many preferred the newer large diameter reel with narrow spools that used only the palm of the hand for a brake. Lines were of horsehair or gut and hooks were similar to today's. Floats of quill and cork were carefully crafted to provide a delicate buoyancy for a natural presentation of the bait.

The continent's first steelhead sports anglers were very likely the pioneers of Vancouver Island. (It is possible that this distinction goes to the first steelheaders at Fort Langley on the Fraser River. In either event, the first steelheaders were undoubtedly of English decent.) Early settlers spread from the Hudson Bay Company trading post at Fort Victoria to the Cowichan River Valley to establish the first agricultural community on the west coast of Canada. Settlers who tamed the wild land in the 1850s were attracted to the valley by its lush farmland and moderate climate. But they also brought with them the zest for angling which was so popular with English gentlemen of the time.

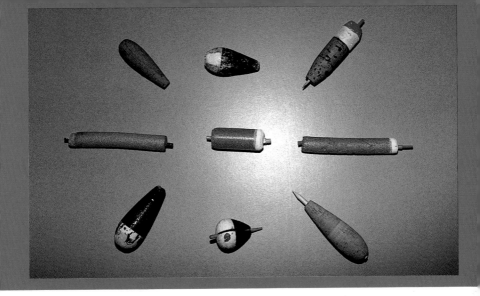

An assortment of home-made floats. Many steelheaders knew the advantages of floats long before commercially manufactured floats were available.

The Cowichan River offered almost unlimited angling opportunities. It held prodigious runs of salmon, trout and winter steelhead. It's a safe bet the Cowichan Valley pioneers began fishing for salmon and steelhead using traditional English angling methods that included float fishing.

Fortunately, we still have among us anglers who can remember the ways of steelheaders as far back as the 1930s. Charlie Stroulger of Duncan, B.C. took his first Cowichan steelhead in 1939. Charlie said that in those days floats were homemade affairs fashioned from cork with a hole drilled through the center and a carved wood pin to hold the line in the float. In many respects those floats were the same as today's. Charlie told me that rods of those days were cane, either hollow or greenheart, from nine to twelve feet in length. Hand-made spoons, roe and baits of cheese coated with Vaseline were the principal attractants of those times. One of the first factory-made lures was the Devon Minnow, a hollow metal tube with wiggling wings.

George Frisky, long-time Vedder River steelheader, remembers fishing the Vedder River in 1932. In those days, his favorite lure was the golf tee. This was made by drilling a hole the length of a red wooden golf tee and passing a wire leader through the hole. A treble hook was fastened to the wire and the lure was ready to fish, with or without added bait. Rods were bamboo, either female, which were hollow in the center, or male, which were solid. The female bamboo was more sensitive and best for light lines, the males were tougher and lasted longer.

The Hardy Silex, an English-manufactured center-pin reel, was the steelheader's first choice, but price considerations restricted many to less

---

A few of the tools available to today's steelheader. The tools have gotten better with every generation but our love of the sport remains a constant.

expensive reels. In the thirties, George earned $4.25 a day as a logger, a Hardy Silex cost around $52.00.

Floats were home-made from cork or ping pong balls. The ping pong ball float was made by drilling a 1/4 inch hole through a ball, and inserting a drinking straw in the hole. The angler's line ran through the straw and was held in place by a carved wood peg. George is credited with being the first steelheader to use wool as an attractant. A pair of bobby sox provided the material George used to begin a way of steelheading we all take for granted today.

In his book, *The Master and His Fish,* Roderick Haig-Brown tells us, "In British Columbia many fishermen use bobbers, adjusting them so that the lead weights bump along the rocks or gravel of the bottom while the lighter bait or lure sweeps along just above. With this rigging, it is possible to cast upstream and get a long reasonably safe drift down past the fisherman." Those observations are from 1971. From that day to this, little has changed in the art of float fishing. Perhaps because the system has neared perfection?

The Advantages of Steelheading With a Float

There are only two ways to fish steelhead—with a float and without. Those who fish without a float, I call bottom bouncers; this is not intended to be a demeaning term. There are times when bottom bouncing is the most effective way to take steelhead, but there are many more times when the float provides an edge that will let you outfish the bottom bouncer.

For years I have suspected that a proficient float angler would outfish an equally proficient bottom bouncer. Logic told me that the advantages of a visual strike indictor, precise lure placement and natural presentation would give a significant edge to steelheaders using a float. I believed this to be so but had no proof, then, one day in the winter of 1993, lady luck provided me with what I consider to be proof.

Through a fortunate coincidence, two friends of mine met on a small river in British Columbia. In many ways these men were alike. Both were steelheading fanatics, both had been steelheaders for more than twenty years, and both were licensed steelhead guides. The primary difference between

As the rivers grow more crowded, steelheaders need an advantage to keep ahead of the pack—floats offer you a leg-up on the competition.

these men was their preferred tackle. One is a British Columbia native who fishes almost exclusively with floats, the other a U.S. angler who prefers bottom bouncing. Both felt their method was superior.

It was one of those magic moments. The river was just dropping into shape. A fresh run of wild steelhead was in and they were biting. All day the two fished together. Both used fresh roe and sand shrimp. From pool to pool they leap-frogged, each giving the other first water in alternating turns. By day's end, these two experts had hooked eight steelhead. The float fisher had hooked seven to the bottom bouncer's one.

As often happens in our sport, there is room for disagreement as to why the float fisher outfished his bottom bouncing companion. The float fisher was more familiar with the stream, and that can be important. Yet, both were experts in reading water and either could have done well the first time they fished any river. My bottom bouncing friend points out that he took the biggest fish that day, but it's clear to me that the float gave my B.C. friend a big advantage.

The float gives steelheaders five advantages over bottom bouncing. In order of importance these are as follows:

1. Floats allow you to fish water that cannot be fished well by the bottom bouncer.
2. Floats provide a visual strike indicator.
3. Floats allow you to precisely position your lure.
4. Floats allow you to control the speed of your lure for a natural presentation.
5. Float anglers have less downtime than bottom bouncers.

Let's take a quick look at each of these important advantages of float fishing.

Fishing Hard to Reach Waters

There are few places the float fisher can reach which the bottom bounc-

er can't. But reaching the water you want to fish and fishing it properly can be two different things. Steelhead often lie in places the bottom bouncer simply cannot fish well. Classic examples of such spots are undercut banks on the far side of the river, the head of pools that lie upstream from the angler, backeddies, and grabby rock gardens.

For a float fisher, undercut banks on the far side of the river are easy pickings. He simply casts to the far bank, reels in until his float is in the heart of the lie and lets it bounce along through the holding water. The bottom bouncer finds this type of water exceedingly hard

Nick Amato works an upstream lie that would be impossible to fish effectively without a float.

to fish as the current will quickly sweep his offering out of the lie.

One of the finest steelhead pools I have ever seen is on a Vancouver Island river. The tail of the pool is accessible. The head is completely hemmed in by steep cliffs, approach is impossible. Bottom bouncers have no alternative but to sling their gear upstream and then reel rapidly as the swift current sweeps their gear back toward them. They find it difficult to detect strikes and lose their gear about every other cast. Float fishers who work this pool have no problems. They simply cast to the head of the pool and take up slack as their float returns toward them. When the float goes under, they know a steelhead has taken the bait.

Back-eddies frustrate bottom bouncers. Steelhead love to lie in the swirling waters but it can be difficult to work a lure in the conflicting currents. Bottom bouncers find that a cast to the portion of the back-eddy moving downstream misses the fish. Conversely, a cast into the swirling water moving upstream, against the current, will not result in a decent drift. This type of water is the float fisher's meat. The float can be cast past the desired drift, reeled back to the perfect lie and let swirl merrily in the back-eddy.

Back-eddies are an excellent place to work a marabou jig under the float. No matter whether the float is bouncing along rapidly on the outer edge of the swirl or drifting lazily in the quiet water, the jig is undulating enticingly.

The author with a small stream steelhead that couldn't resist a pink marabou jig swirling in a back-eddy, beneath a float.

The boulder-strewn rock garden is a mixed blessing for the bottom bouncer. Steelhead have an affinity for this type of water. Bottom bouncers know that the best of these runs have a voracious appetite for tackle. After losing three or four leaders and lures, many bottom bouncers move on. These areas are no problem for float fishers. Once the float is correctly adjusted to swing your offering just above the boulders, you will lose no tackle. Floats let you work prime waters that bottom bouncers may fish only at a high price in lost time and tackle.

The Visual Strike Indicator

Steelhead frequently are delicate biters. There are exceptions of course,

---

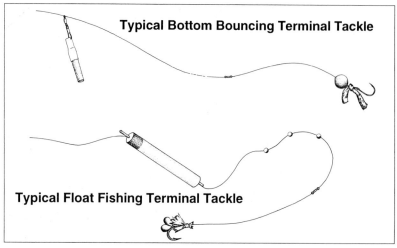

Typical Bottom Bouncing Terminal Tackle

Typical Float Fishing Terminal Tackle

like the summer run that streaks across the pool to slam your spinner, but far more often the bite of a steelhead is barely descernible. It's frequently mistaken for the nibbling of small trout. Veteran bottom bouncers tell neophytes that the difference between the top rods and the rest of the pack is the ability to tell the difference between the bounce of pencil lead on the rocks and the subtle tug of a steelhead. How frustrating it can be to fish all day without a hookup then to miss the day's only strike because we thought our lure was hung on the bottom. It has happened to all of us when bottom bouncing. This is seldom a problem for the float fisher.

A properly weighted float will dip under with the slightest pressure. If your float is properly weighted and the distance from float to lure has been

properly adjusted, strikes are easily detected. Even the tentative take of a lethargic cold water fish will make your float scream "strike!" It's as simple as that. When the float goes under—strike! That's a concept a six year old perch angler fully understands.

Precisely Positioning Your Lure

Your float tells you exactly where your lure is. If you see a seam you want to fish, simply cast your float upstream from the head of the seam and to the far side of it. Then reel in until the float is exactly

Three steelheaders work a quiet pool on the Quatse River. Note that the anglers can easily position their floats exactly where they wish simply by casting past the desired lie and reeling in until the float is in the sweet spot.

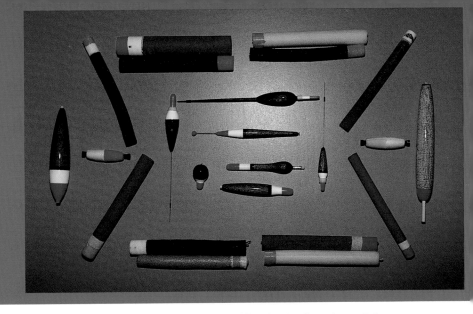

A selection of modern floats. Note they all feature brilliantly painted tops that mark the proper water line and serve as visible strike indicators.

where you want it. From there, you simply free spool as you walk the float down the seam. Bottom bouncers can only guess where their lure is. They can see their line entering the water but must estimate the distance and angle between the lure and the place the line enters the water. Often the lure is a good distance from where the bottom bouncer thinks it is. Even if the bottom bouncer knows exactly where their bait is, they may be hard pressed to keep it in the drift they wish. The current tugging on the line tends to sweep it across the river rather than in a straight line down the seam.

Controlling the Speed of Your Presentation

As often as not, float anglers simply let the float move along at the speed the currents dictate. On occasion that's exactly the right speed to attract a strike. But not always.

In pools and runs more than four feet deep, there is a significant difference in current speed from the top of the water to the bottom. Friction, bottom structure and other factors of stream physics decrease the current speed near the bottom. The deeper the water, the more significant the difference between top and bottom current speeds. In a ten-foot-deep run your float may be perking along at five knots while the current near the bottom, where steelhead lie, may be less than two knots. If you simply let your float zip along at the speed of the surface current, your lure will move through the strike zone at more than twice the speed of the current where the fish lie. This results in a very unnatural presentation that will seldom bring a strike and often may spook the fish.

Float fishers can readily control the speed of their lure. If you wish to let the surface current dictate your presentation speed, simply free spool and let the current do the work. Conversely, you can hold back the float as it walks downstream to fish as slowly as you wish. If you want, you can fish a pool at several speeds perhaps learning what speed of presentation the fish want that day.

Like all other aspects of steelheading, there are no fixed rules. Steelhead may want a rapid presentation one day and a slower one the next. Floats give you the ability to fully control your lure speed.

Bottom bouncers have a hard time duplicating the natural drift of a float. Each time their weight hits bottom, their lure pauses in an unnatural manner. There are times when such a bounce and pause presentation is just the ticket to trigger a steelhead into striking. But when a more natural presentation is needed, the bottom bouncer is at a disadvantage.

Limiting Down Time

The more time your lure is in the water, the more fish you catch. That's an inarguable fact. Another inarguable fact is that bottom bouncers spend a good bit of their fishing time re-rigging. Float fishers do not. Guess who spends the most time with their lure in the water? In recent times bottom bouncers have found some new tools that help reduce hang-ups. Slinkys and

the new precision release leads both limit hang-ups. Yet, on many of our boulder-strewn rivers, the best of the bottom bouncers lose several leaders an hour. Time spent re-rigging cuts into valuable fishing time and constant re-rigging can be extraordinarily frustrating when cold fingers are uncooperative.

Even when tackle losses are small, the bottom bouncer who uses bait is at a disadvantage to the float fisher. The constant beating bait takes as it bounces along the bottom requires frequent re-baiting. The float fisher's baits last longer. In a day, this difference can be considerable; in a season, it can be huge.

Bottom bouncing in boulder gardens such as this can cost a leader a cast. This is ideal float water. A float will allow a snag free drift that can be precisely controlled to work all the prime holding area.

Float Fishing Tackle

Floats

Obviously, every float angler must have a float. But there's far more to float fishing than simply attaching a red and white plastic bobber to your usual drift fishing gear. To fish floats effectively you must have a complete system of rod, reel, float, weights and terminal tackle, all balanced to work in harmony.

There is no one best float for steelheading, just as there is no one best rod, reel, or lure. Selecting the proper float requires that you give consideration to the type of water you will be fishing, and the weight of the lure or bait you will present for the steelhead's inspection.

Two of the best steelhead floats are the simple foam floats widely used in British Columbia, known as "dink" floats, and the balsa floats commonly used in the Great Lakes region. Both share the attributes of being infinitely and rapidly adjustable and both come in a sufficient variety of sizes and

A selection of balsa floats manufactured by Mick Thill. Top quality floats such as these are now available to fit any conditions you may encounter.

shapes to suit almost any steelheading situation.

The dink float is inexpensive and can easily be modified to suit almost any water condition. Most dink floats are four to six inches in length, approximately one-half-inch in diameter and feature a brightly painted top for ease of visibility. Favorite colors are red and chartreuse, red is most easily seen in low light conditions and chartreuse is best in the middle of the day.

Most dink floats are threaded onto the line via a center tunnel or angled tubes at each end of the float. Center tunnel tubes are held in place either by a toothpick or with a bamboo reed that comes with the float. Floats with angled tubes at top and bottom rely on a wrap of line around the float to create sufficient friction to hold the float in place.

The long cylindrical foam floats are known as "dink" floats. These are very popular in British Columbia and are rapidly catching on in the U.S.

In British Columbia, where dink floats are part of every steelheaders arsenal, tackle shops display bins of dink floats in every size and color. In the U.S. dink floats are just beginning to catch on. Mr Ed' floats, manufactured by Ed Larm of Camas WA., are now available in large tackle shops throughout the Northwest. Ed manufactrues several small dink floats that are ideal for light line and jig fishing.

Balsa floats are the most lovely of the floats and many prefer the buoyancy of balsa over foam. Balsa floats are pleasure to fish, and they are a often beautifully finished. The top manufacturer of balsa floats in North America is Mick Thill. Born in Chicago, Mick moved to England as a teenager, there he studied under the continent's best anglers and began a career as a competition match angler.

For twenty-six years Mick was one of Europe's top competition match anglers. Mick has won five world angling championships. When he returned to the U.S. Mick designed a series of balsa floats that are now marketed by Lindy-Little Joe, Inc. of Brainerd, Minnesota.

Mick's floats come in a variety of sizes ranging from the dime sized River Master to the six inch Big Fish Slider. For whatever conditions you encounter Mick has a float to fill the bill. Many of his floats are designed to be quickly interchangeable and most are held to the line by silicone sleeves that can quickly be removed to change floats. These floats are hand-crafted

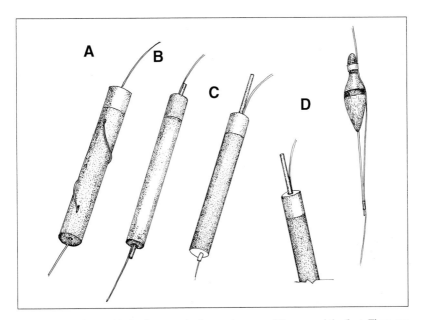

A. This float relies on friction between the float and a wrap of line around the float. These are very easy to rig and fairly easy to adjust, but you must have slack line to make an adjustment in either direction.
B. This float features center tunnel and a bamboo stick. The line is held against the inside of the tunnel by the stick. These floats are very easy to adjust and easy to rig. On occasion the bamboo swells until it is too big to use.
C. This is the most common float used in British Columbia. The line passes through a center tunnel and is held in place by a flat toothpick. (The round ones don't work very well). This float is easy to adjust and very easy to rig. If you run out of toothpicks, a twig will substitute.
D. The Thill floats are held in place by two small pieces of rubber tubing. This system is very easily adjusted and easy to rig. You must be sure to carry a supply of tubing material as these floats cannot be used without it.

in a process that involves more than twenty separate steps. The top of each Thill float is painted with two bands of bright color. The top band of red marks the ideal water level for fishing quiet waters. The bottom of the yellow band marks the proper float height for fast water.

Rods

The ideal rod for float fishing steelhead is largely a matter of personal preference. However, most would agree the ideal float rod is between ten and fourteen feet in length. It has a fast action tip to allow it to load up rapidly for casting, a strong backbone for battling big steelhead, and, above all, will be light enough to cast from daylight to dark without unduly fatiguing the angler. Until the arrival of modern graphite, no rod came close to this ideal. Now we have so many choices of fine rods that we should always be able to find the ideal rod for our circumstances.

Those not accustomed to float fishing usually question the need for such long rods. Once you have fished with floats for a short while, the value of long rods will become apparent. The primary need for long rods is to allow casting the float and as much as eight feet of line and leader. Obviously, it would be impossible to cast a float line and leader combination eight feet in length with a seven-foot rod.

The second benefit of the long rods is line control, to help keep the line above the water, to help work the line around and over obstacles, and to control the speed of the float. If you can keep the line from touching the water between your rod tip and the float, setting the hook is an easy matter. However, if you have a long length of line laying on the water with a large belly in the line, it will be almost impossible to quickly set the hook.

Another advantage of long rods is the ability to steer and control the speed of the float. On many small streams and in parts of large rivers you will find that casting is unnecessary if you have a long enough rod. You can steer the float exactly where you want it simply by pointing your rod tip. You can also control the speed of the float's progress if you can keep the rod tip directly in line with the course of the float.

Because float fishing for steelhead has been slow to catch on in the U.S.A., Canadian anglers have more float rods to choose from than do their U.S. counterparts. But this is changing rapidly. Until recently no U.S. manufacturer sold rods designed specifically for steelhead float fishing. Today, G. Loomis offers an assortment of nine float rods. Lamiglas, Fenwick and Lindy-Little Joe, Inc. also market float rods.

The Lindy-Little Joe, Inc. float rod is the only rod they carry. It is a three-piece twelve foot three inch graphite rod that weighs only five-and-one-half ounces. This rod, designed by Mick Thill, is designed for lines up to five pound test. It is ideal for gentle rivers and any situation where light lines can be used.

Reels

All reels currently used by steelheaders have a place in the float fisher's arsenal. The commonly used level wind or bait casting reels are prevalent among west coast float fishers and spinning reels have their followers, but the serious float anglers in British Columbia and the Great Lakes have an affinity for the center-pin reel.

Spinning reels find their place in the float fisher's arsenal primarily with those who fish light lures and light lines. A deadly steelheading combo, effective in quiet water and swift runs, is the float and jig combination. Many anglers prefer a spinning reel for this type of fishing because the small floats used with jigs as light as one sixteenth ounce can be most easily cast with a

Stanton
4 1/4" by Cliff Adock

Pacific Steelheader
4 1/2" by Islander

"Searun"
4 1/2" by Islander

Coult
3 3/4" by Ron Coult

MacDonald
3 3/4" by Norm MacDonald

MacDonald
4 1/2" by
Norm MacDonald

Clough
by Derek Clough

Eagle
4 5/8" by Vivan

**Avon Royal
Supreme**
4 5/8" by Grice & Young

Purist
4 1/2" by J.W. Young

Hardy Supurba
4" Precision to Silex

Hardy Silex
4" by Hardy Bros.

This is a selection of center-pin reels from Fred Helmer's collection.

spinning reel. In any situation where your float, weights, and lure total less than one quarter ounce a spinning reel is a fine choice.

All major manufacturers offer high quality spinning reels that will serve nicely. Spinning reels with three or more ball bearings are usually the smoothest and most reliable. Rear drag models offer the smoothest drag system, but recently some top of the line spinning reels have featured top of the spool drag systems that work quite well. When selecting a spinning reel look for a model that is properly counter-balanced to avoid wobbling when reeling in line. Because the spinning reel is used with light line applications you should limit your spinning reels to the smaller models weighing six ounces or less, with a line capacity of approximately 150 yards of eight pound test line.

The standard of the west coast steelheader, be they bottom bouncers or float fishers, is the level wind, bait casting reel. As with spinning reels, there are a handful of quality manufacturers and dozens of models to suit your needs. Today many models are marketed in exotic finishes or with sleek aerodynamic styling. While these may look racy, they offer no advantage over the simple round reels such as the Abu Garcia 5000 and the Shimano Bantams that have proven reliability. My choice would be a reel with three or more ball bearings and a line capacity of approximately 250 yards of fifteen pound test line. If the budget will allow, you might wish to purchase one smaller reel for light tackle angling and a larger one for fishing big waters.

The center-pin reel is by far the favorite of the serious British Columbia and Great Lakes steelheader. This may be because it casts more smoothly than other reels, or because the direct drive reels require more skill on the anglers part than a reel with gears. Or it may simply be a badge of competency that announces that this angler is a serious steelheader.

The center-pin reel is both good and bad and can only be judged by each of us individually. On the positive side these reels are extraordinarily smooth casting. They are usually quite nicely finished, and they allow you to free spool your float with almost no drag. On the negative side they can be the devil to learn to cast. The lack of gears makes it difficult to catch up to a fish that is running toward you and likewise they retrieve line more slowly than a typical reel with gears. This can cost a steelheader a good deal of time during a full day's angling. In addition, they are usually expensive. Still there's nothing quite the same as palming a single action reel while a big steelhead races downstream, then reeling frantically to catch up when the fish reverses course.

Weighting the Float

There are as many ways to weight a float system as the imagination allows, but all have these important attributes; the float must be weighted so that it protrudes only slightly above the water, and the lure must work its

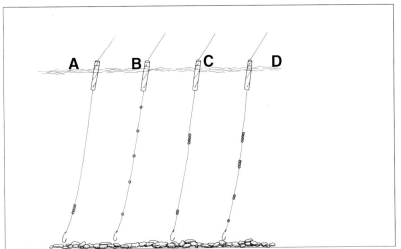

A. *Bulk Shot Method: This is used in heavy current and colored water. The concentration of weights will keep the lure near the bottom. This method casts well but may spook fish in very clear water.*

B. *Equal Distance Method: This method tends to allow the line to sweep with the current in a uniform arc. This weighing system casts quite well.*

C. *Double Distance: This method keeps the majority of the weight above the fish's plane of vision. Weights must be at least twice as far apart as the distance between the bottom weight and the lure. If not tangles will result.*

D. *Multiplier: This system calls for incremental weighting with each set of weights larger than the predecessor. This system has the greatest weight near the top where the current is heavier and the least weight near the bottom where currents are light.*

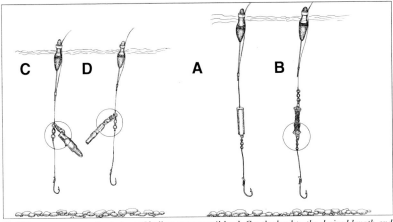

A. *This system uses a short piece of hollow-core pencil lead. Cut the lead to the desired length and slip the main line through the lead before tying on the swivel.*

B. *A slinky can be used with a float by clipping a snap swivel on each end. To change slinkys simply unsnap the swivels and replace the slinky with one of the desired size.*

C. *Standard pencil lead or (Precision Release) leads can be rigged as illustrated to slide freely on the main line. If they are rigged with a snap swivel leads can easily be replaced.*

D. *Many bottom bouncers stick with their old system of weighting when they use floats. They make no change to their usual weighting system other than adding the float above the weight.*

Float Fishing Tackle

magic somewhere between one foot and two feet above the river bottom. How those attributes are achieved is less important than assuring that those two imperatives are met.

The weights used to properly balance a float are usually split shot ranging in size from the largest magnum shot to fine dust. Shot are ideal weights as they can be added and deleted as needed until the float sits properly in the water. In recent years many float anglers have experimented with small eared sinkers that have the added benefit of rapid removal and they may be reused repeatedly. The rubber cored removable sinkers also work well. If you carry three sizes, you can quickly adjust to almost any water condition.

When weighting your float with multiple split shot, eared weights or other systems using multiple weights it is important that you space the weight correctly to avoid tangles. A single group of weights works well as do several equally spaced weights. Two weights separated by a foot or more of monofilament form an unstable aerodynamic which almost guarantees tangles. If you opt for two weights or two sets of weights be sure that the distance between the weights is at least twice as far as the distance between the lower weight and the lure.

Other weighing systems including pencil lead, slinkys and hollow core lead, have all proven satisfactory.

Leaders

Leaders used beneath floats run the gamut from twenty pound test to one pound test and from fourteen inches long to eight feet long. In the big colored waters of western rivers, short heavy leaders work well and are often necessary to land big fish in fast water. In the more gentle waters of Great Lakes rivers it is usually necessary to go to long light leaders to draw a strike.

Leaders should be attached to the main line with a swivel. Top quality ball bearing swivels will eliminate line twist which can be a problem especially when fishing with rotating lures such as Flash and Spins, Birdy Drifters, and Spin-N-Glows. Ultra light leaders of three pound test or less are commonly attached directly to the main line without a swivel.

Abrasion resistant, nonvisible material is usually best for leaders. Maxima Ultra Green, Ande Tournament and Berkley XT are all excellent choices, when fishing with long light leaders. Berkley XL and others especially formulated for limpness are ideal.

Terminal Tackle

Your choice of bait or lure to be fished beneath the float is almost limitless. Because a properly rigged float assures that your offering will stay in

Yvonne Munson proudly proves that Vedder River steelhead love plastic worms fished beneath a float. In late winter the pink worm is the favorite choice of many savvy steelheaders.

the strike zone, buoyant lures such as those preferred by bottom bouncers are unnecessary. However, if you have an affinity for the brightly colored cork lures you will find they can be adapted to fish well beneath floats. Floats seem perfectly adapted to fragile baits such as roe, sand shrimp and worms. The gentle ride provided by the float helps keep these baits on the hook much longer than other techniques.

Artificial lures also fish well beneath the float. Jigs have been used extensively by float anglers working deep quiet pools.

Recently, many steelheaders have learned that the jig and float combination is a deadly tool for probing fast moving water as well. Usually no additional weight is needed when fishing with a lead head jig. Mr. Ed's N.A.S. dink float and a one quarter ounce jig make a beautiful match for low water steelhead. This combination is so light that many prefer to fish it with a spinning reel.

The entire gamut of artificial baits including Jensen Eggs, Gooey Bobs and rubber grubs and worms all fish well beneath a float. These seem to work best in swift water where the chop on the surface causes the lure to dance alluringly. In British Columbia many anglers swear by the combination of a float and small pink, or red rubber worms. It's a combination that looks strange, but has proven its effectiveness in many rivers for many years.

A steelheader's favorite moment—first cast on a lovely run all to yourself.

Fishing With a Float

Now that you have selected a balanced float fishing system, the only thing that stands between you and a steelhead is putting the theories to practice. Let's spend a day on the river. We will look at some common steelheading situations and the tricks used by top rods to take steelhead with a float.

The Classic Steelhead Pool

Most small rivers and streams have several well-defined runs, classic steelhead water with a riffle or cataract at the head, a deep slot, frequently in the middle of the run, and a tailout that shallows into the next riffle. Typically these classic runs are well known to the local steelheading fraternity and are, of course, heavily fished.

If you have the luxury of fishing such a run in solitude, you can fish it methodically and in concert with the water conditions. If not, you will have to adjust your approach to fit in with the other anglers. First, let's suppose you have this fine run all to yourself.

Begin at the head of the pool where the white water cascades into the run. First, estimate the depth at the upper end of the run and adjust your float accordingly. Make your first cast into the white water just where it enters the pool, at the near side of the run. No matter that this water is shallower than the upper part of the run. Before your gear can touch bottom, the current will have swept it into the deeper holding water. Let the float free spool down the run for about fifty feet, then reel in and adjust your float, if necessary. If it was dragging bottom, as evidenced by the head of the float pointing downstream, shorten up a bit. If your gear never touched bottom, you may want to lengthen your float-to-lure distance until you know your offering is very near bottom.

Frequently the head of a pool will have a deep pocket gouged out by the white water entering the run. This pocket may be the best holding water in the run. Don't leave until you have fished it thoroughly. If the head of the pool provides swirling back-eddies, work these well. Let your float swirl all around until you are certain every fish in the pocket has had a good chance to see your offering.

Remember that deep water has a much faster current on the surface than on the bottom. When working water more than four feet deep, you will want to consider this factor and alter your presentation to slow your lure's speed to match the current flow near the bottom. To do this, you need to hold back your float's downstream progress so that it slowly walks down the run.

If the surface current is quite rapid, you may need to alter your terminal gear to work your lure slowly through the lie. The first modification is to

Small streams can be much easier to read than larger rivers. This angler has correctly surmised that fish should be holding in the deeper water near the far bank.

add two small split shot near the lure to hold it down. The rapid current will be pushing hard against your line and leader. If your line and leader are not weighted heavily enough, holding back your float will cause the current to push them up toward the surface. The added weight needed to resist the current flow may require a switch to a more buoyant float.

You will also need to lengthen your float-to-lure distance to keep the lure in the strike zone. Even with the addition of extra weight, the current will try to sweep your lure to the surface as you hold back on the float. An additional foot or two of depth will allow for some upward curvature in your leader while keeping your lure in the steelhead's face.

Now that you have re-rigged to fish the deep water with a natural presentation, find a casting position that lets you stay in line with your float. Obviously, you cannot hold back an upstream cast, nor can you do so with a cast directly cross-stream from your position. Ideally, you want to be upstream from the lie and in a direct line with it.

Often, the deep runs are below points, snags, river bends and man-made obstructions, such as bridge abutments. In these cases posi-

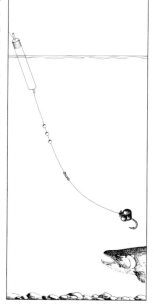

Your lure must be presented at the proper depth and at the proper speed to consistently trigger strikes.

Float Fishing for Steelhead

With a long rod you can position yourself to guide your float down the edge of a seam. This churning run has two distinct seams—both should be carefully worked.

tion yourself above, and in line with, the desired drift. If there is no way to get in position to hold back your float, consider the bottom bouncing float fishing method described in the chapter on advanced techniques. (See page 54)

When you have thoroughly fished the head of the pool, move down about thirty feet and begin again. From this point make your casts upstream so that you are overlapping the casts you made from the head of the pool by ten feet or so. You may find that you need to shorten your float as the water in the middle of the run might be a bit shallower than the head. Be certain you cover every part of the run that might hold fish. I often begin with a cast to the near side of the run then extend each cast by a foot or two until the entire run is covered from near side to far and from head to tail.

If you are convinced fish are present, change bait or lures and fish the entire run again. Often, something as simple as changing from salmon eggs to sand shrimp or a switch to a spinner will trigger a strike from a fish that has spurned your previous offering.

Be certain you have worked the run from head to tail and side to side. Steelhead seldom move more than a few feet to take a lure, therefore you must be certain you have covered every square yard of the run before moving on. All of us have had the disheartening experience of working a run for half an hour and moving on only to have another angler move in and take a fish behind us. Sometimes this happens because the second angler has a lure that tweaked the steelhead's fancy, but, as often as not, the second angler's success was simply attributable to the fact they put their offering right on the nose of a fish that you didn't cover.

Finally, work down to the tailout. If fish are on the move, this may be the most productive water in the run. Again, you want to adjust your depth

The author shows the result of patiently sweeping a tailout with a float. This fish was holding in a broad tailout in less than three feet of water. Floats are deadly in this type of water.

to keep your offering just above the bottom. You want to methodically work every possible square yard of holding water. As your float approaches the end of the run, it will start dragging on the bottom because the tailout is the shallowest part of the pool. You can avoid hang-ups and tantalize many a steelhead into striking by holding back the float as it approached the tailout. This will cause your lure to raise in the water column as the drag of the current pushes against your line. Your float and its payload will sweep toward your side of the river while the lure lifts and swings in front of the fish. This sudden up and across sweeping motion often triggers a strike.

In our hypothetical situation, you had the run entirely to yourself. If you have to share the water with other anglers, you will want to change your tactics. A popular bumper sticker advises, "Life is uncertain. Eat dessert first." A steelheader's credo might be similar—"Life is uncertain. Fish the tailout first." If you expect others to arrive before you have finished the run, by all means, work the tailout first.

Tailouts are prime water, especially when the river is dropping. Don't be caught working the head of the pool when the next group arrives and starts whacking fish in the tailout.

If you decide to work the tailout first, approach with caution. Approach quietly and stay out of the water, if possible. These shallow water steelhead are usually spooky as they are often in water very near the edge of their comfort zone.

Working a Fish

All too often we see the float go down and pop back up, before our mind registers what's happening. If you miss a strike, carefully note the

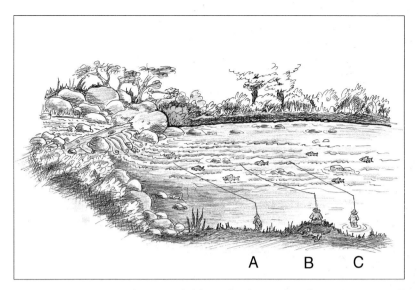

A   B   C

Note that the casts from each position slightly overlap the casts from the previous position. If you have the run to yourself, fish it from A to C. If you expect company, begin at C. Keep your casts' drifts under seventy-five feet long. Move as many times as necessary to cover the entire run carefully.

exact spot where your float went down. You have now solved a major piece of the steelhead puzzle. You know where a steelhead is, and perhaps of greater importance, you have found a steelhead that is in a biting mood. You should be able to catch that fish.

The first step is to do what you were doing. Cast the float so that it passes directly over the spot where the strike occurred. To do this you need to understand a bit about currents and steelhead behavior. In most water that holds steelhead, your offering hasn't fully sunk and started drifting naturally until the float has drifted five to ten feet. This distance depends on the speed of the current, the depth of the run, and the type lead you are using. Also remember that frequently steelhead drift along beneath your lure for several feet before striking. Therefore, your next cast needs to be at least fifteen feet upstream from where the strike came. Make your next cast twenty feet upstream from the strike and a little farther toward the far bank than necessary. Reel in until the float is directly on line with the fish and let it slip over the fish. This time pay attention!

If you have made a half dozen casts to the fish with no result, change baits or lures. When in doubt, go a bit smaller. If you began with salmon eggs, go to sand shrimp or vice versa. If you began with a rubber worm, drop down to a Gooey Bob or even a single Jensen Egg. A steelhead that bit once usually comes back to a slightly different color or size lure. Don't leave that spot until you have shown that fish at least three different baits or lures and have presented them at several different depths. The fish may need a bit of a rest before it will bite again, but odds are that fish will bite again.

British Columbia steelhead guides often fish with their clients. When the guide's float goes down, they purposely fail to set the hook. Instead, they instruct their client to cast to the spot where their float went down. This trick has saved the day for many a guide.

On the Nanaimo River, I once saw the same steelhead hooked three times in a thirty minute period. The first strike came on a rubber worm, but didn't result in a hookup. My partner re-rigged with a single Jensen Egg and hooked the fish on his third cast. Unfortunately, it came unbuttoned after about fifteen seconds and one fine leap. We took a coffee break for twenty minutes then came back after the fish with fresh salmon eggs. Three casts later, we had the small wild buck that was kept for hatchery brood stock.

Pocket Water Float Fishing

Pocket water, the bane of bottom bouncers, is a float fisher's favorite water. Small pockets gouged behind boulders, swept from the feet of root wads and carved from the bedrock of streams are the stuff of steelheader's dreams. But these dreams can turn to nightmares when pocket water is fished with bottom bouncing gear. Lost tackle and frustration over the inability to keep the lure in the pocket keep many steelheaders from enjoying pocket water. The float has changed all that.

Classic pocket water is often associated with small streams where limited water depth forces the fish into the few pockets that provide enough cover to satisfy their instinct for hiding. Yet many large rivers have small pockets that have all the attributes of small stream pocket water.

The first twenty-plus-pound steelhead I ever fought, (I choose my words carefully here, as the steelhead won that battle) came from a bathtub

Don't pass up pocket water. One or two casts to each likely lie will tell you if fish are present. Be prepared. Things happen fast in pocket water.

In pocket water small slots and seams created by boulders and other obstructions provide the only possible steelhead lies. Be sure to work both sides of the seams created by the boulders, and work quickly. Two to five casts to each seam is sufficient.

sized pocket in a large river. For over a quarter mile the river ran wide, shallow and fast. Nowhere was the water deep enough to comfort a steelhead, yet near the center of the river a boulder shouldered above the water, and behind that boulder was a pocket the size of an old fashioned bathtub. There was no way to fish the pocket except with a float. If I had cast bottom bouncing gear into the pocket, the immense drag of the current on the long line would have swept the lure through the pocket in a flash. There was nothing to it with a float. A long cast, purposely beyond and upstream from the pocket, put the float just where it needed to be. By reeling in a bit of slack, the float was positioned directly in line with the boulder. As the float swept toward the boulder, the current pushed it to my side of the pocket, riding just on the edge of the seam formed by the rushing water and the backeddy behind the rock. The float was less than five feet downstream from the boulder when it swooped under and the battle began.

Since that day, I have seen floats work their magic in pockets many anglers would never try to fish. Pocket picking is my favorite steelheading. Once you try it with a float, you too will be hooked.

You need to make a few modifications to your float gear to successfully pick pockets. Use larger floats, more weight and shorter leaders; leaders of twelve to fifteen inches are about right. Be prepared to make no more than a half dozen casts to each pocket before moving on. One good trick is to have two terminal rigs ready to use. Fish the first rig—maybe a rubber worm—for a few casts, then switch to your second favorite rig for a few more casts before moving on. Because most pockets are small and fast flowing, it's important that your lure reach the strike zone rapidly. This requires a heavy shot string or lead.

The rapid choppy water in a typical pocket often submerges a float weighted for slower water. To assure that you don't lose sight of your float, use a larger float, one that will ride high while carrying the heavy string of shot needed to get the lure down fast.

Everything that has to do with pocket water fishing happens fast. Flip your float upstream from the pocket and rapidly reel in until the float is headed for the heart of the pocket. If you have positioned your float properly, it will sweep along the near edge of the pocket. Actual fishing time will be about five seconds. Stay alert. Things happen quickly—if at all. Pocket water steelhead usually take on the first cast or two.

If you don't get a take on the first cast, fire the float back out there. This time work it down the heart of the pocket. For pockets behind boulders cast just beyond the boulder, then quickly pull the float toward yourself so that it slips into the calm water behind the boulder. Let it swirl around in the back-eddy for a few seconds before the current takes it away.

If no strike comes, work the float down the far side of the pocket. Again, stay alert. The float will be in prime water only a few seconds. Strikes come fast. It's easy to roll a fish without getting a good hookset if you aren't on your toes. Quickly sweep your float away from the tail of the pocket before it hangs-up in the shallows.

Most classic pocket water provides a lot of water that is too shallow to hold fish, sprinkled with small pockets that may hold fish. If you want to cover all possible holding water, you need to work quickly. Unless you are certain there is a fish in the pocket you are working, make four or five casts and move on. That way you can cover several miles of pocket water in a day's fishing. If there are fresh fish moving in the river, you should find them if you work fast and cover a lot of water.

Top lures for picking pockets are pink rubber worms, Gooey-Bobs, Jensen eggs and small yarn balls. My favorite is the rubber worm. Pocket water steelhead can't seem to resist a rubber worm. Fresh baits such as salmon eggs and sand shrimp work well but the rough treatment they receive in boisterous pocket water is very hard on fragile baits. You may find you need to re-bait every two or three casts.

Still Water Float Fishing

Many steelheaders never have the chance to fish steelhead in still water, but the opportunity does arise. Perhaps the most heavily fished steelhead water in the world, the confluence of Washington's Blue Creek and the Cowlitz River is one such place. The mouth of the Methow River where it empties into the Columbia is another. In these locales and many others, the float offers such an obvious advantage that even Northwest steelheaders have abandoned traditional bottom bouncing gear in favor of floats.

Many still water, or nearly still water, steelheading areas feature deep water and heavy concentrations of steelhead that may be holding well above the bottom. This is an ideal situation for the float fishing steelheader.

Still water that is less than eight feet deep may be fished well with traditional fixed floats, however, often these quiet waters run from ten to forty feet deep. These conditions call for a slip float. The chapter on advanced techniques (see page 54) covers rigging and casting slip floats. For now we will presume a complete understanding of the mechanics of slip float angling.

Still waters are best fished with light lines, small floats and lures that provide a strong visual stimuli without the benefit of movement provided by strong current flows. Light lines are necessary because clear water and slow moving lures give steelhead ample opportunity to examine our offering.

Small floats are used because there is no need for the buoyancy required to keep the float visible in choppy water. Another reason for small floats is their increased sensitivity. still water steelhead often nibble delicately, so delicately the bite is barely discernible. Tiny floats telegraph these tiny bites.

Still water steelheading occurs in quiet pools on rivers with gentle gradients or at the junction where small rivers join larger ones. Floats are a definite advantage in still water.

Almost any bait or lure works beneath a still water float but lures should be capable of providing an alluring action with no assist from the current. Nothing does this better than marabou. By far the most popular still water steelhead lure is the marabou jig.

Many still water float fishers use an outfit something like this: An eight-foot rod designed for six to eight pound test line, spinning reel filled with six pound line, small slip float, and a one quarter or three-eighths ounce marabou jig. Favorite jig colors are pink, pink and white, black and purple. Many experts use a small piece of shrimp meat on the hook of their jig to add flavor and scent.

Still waters have little in the way of seams, riffles, or other surface markers to provide a hint as to what's beneath, but you can still do a bit of detective work to find the lay of the pool. As with moving water, use your float as a depth indicator. Simply keep lengthening the distance from float to lure until you know how deep the area is.

Steelhead in deep, still water are not always oriented with the bottom as is common in flowing water. One day you may find the fish quite near the

bottom of a twenty foot deep pool, the next day they may be near the bottom at the six foot depth and yet another day they will be suspended ten feet deep in twenty feet of water. Trial and error, keen observation of others, and sharing of information with other anglers will help you learn at what depth they are.

Even in relatively still water, subtle currents and wind move your float. It's a good idea to keep your reel in free spool while applying slight tension on the spool with your thumb, then let your float slowly slip downstream or as the wind dictates. If circumstances require an upstream cast, slowly retrieve line as the wind and current push the float back toward you. It is imperative that you keep all

A neophyte steelheader receives a bit of advice from an expert. Good advice can be invaluable, but nothing beats spending lots of time on the river.

Float Fishing for Steelhead

slack out of the line and watch your float like a hawk.

Still water steelhead often take the lure very gently. Many times the pick-up is signaled by a slight lift of the float as the fish releases the tension on the line by mouthing the jig, other times the only indication that a fish is present is a slight jiggling of your float. You must learn to strike very quickly when these tentative strikes occur. If you wait too long, the fish will drop the bait. If the float is lifting up, jiggling or, best of all, is fully under water—strike!

If you miss the chance to strike, don't despair. still water steelhead often return to your jig as long as a bit of bait remains. This time be ready and strike the instant the float does anything that says "fish."

Still water steelhead are affected by changes in barometric pressure, much like bass. When a cold front passes through with a dropping barometer, they often go off the bite or become very tentative biters. Fishing usually improves in stable weather.

Nothing improves your float fishing skills like time on the river. In this chapter you have been given a rudimentary glimpse at techniques used by the top rods on three typical steelheading situations. Almost every type of water you encounter will be similar to one of the three situations covered in this chapter. Now it's time to spend time on the river putting these techniques to work.

Reading Water

Back to the basics again. You can't catch a fish that isn't there. Conversely, an undisturbed steelhead can usually be caught. Simple, isn't it? The first step toward steelheading success is finding the fish. Occasionally, you can see steelhead in their lie. That's wonderful. When you can spot an undisturbed steelhead, cast to your quarry, and succeed in hooking it, you have experienced one of steelheading's higher joys. Unfortunately, only a small minority of steelhead are seen before they are hooked. Most of your steelheading will be devoted to fishing where you think steelhead ought to be. With a little practice, you can use the clues found on the water's surface to make accurate guesses about the steelhead's whereabouts. Learning to interpret these clues is known as reading water.

It has been said ad nauseam that 10 percent of the anglers catch 90 percent of the fish. That's probably an overstatement, but not by much. Perhaps a more important, and also totally unscientific, statistic is that 90 percent of the steelhead are found in 10 percent of the river. The small cadre of anglers who catch most of the steelhead know which 10 percent of the river is most likely to hold steelhead. The top rods undoubtedly have other well honed skills, but there is no avoiding the fact that you can't catch a steelhead unless

Chart 1. Normal Steelhead Distribution
Based on Water Depth (Assuming Normal Winter Flow)

Percent of Steelhead in River

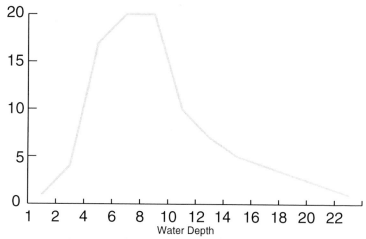

Water Depth

The primary concentrations of steelhead will hold in water between three and ten feet deep. In average conditions more than seventy percent of all steelhead in the river will be found in such water.

Chart 2. Normal Steelhead Distribution
Based Upon Current Flow (Assuming Normal Winter Flow)
Percent of Steelhead in River

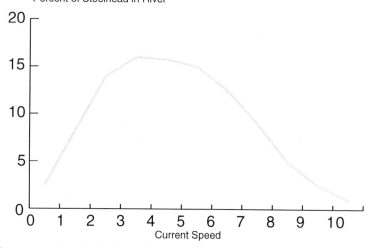

Current Speed

The majority of steelhead will hold in currents between two and five knots. Normally such water will hold more than 60% of all steelhead. Conversely, water with a current less than one or more than seven knots will hold less than 25% of the steelhead.

you fish where they are. If you understand their needs, you can often predict where steelhead are holding. Steelhead have evolved to survive in the highly dangerous environment they inhabit, not through intelligence, but by an instinctive wariness. When a native steelhead has successfully returned to the river, it has beaten very high odds. Its success is due to good instincts. These instincts, shared by all wild steelhead, cause one steelhead to act much like another. Good steelhead-holding lies can be compared to the best seats in a theater. There may not always be someone in the seat, but if there's a good crowd, you know which seats will be occupied.

Spawning is the steelhead's primary goal. On the way to that goal steelhead seek water that provides life's three essentials—safety, food, and comfort (comfort relates to current speed, oxygen needs, and water temperature). Water that fully meets all of these needs will hold steelhead. (If the theater is full.) If only two of the three needs are met steelhead may be present. If none of these needs are met, steelhead will be present only briefly as they pass through to more suitable water. When a steelheader can recognize the surface features that tell them where these three essentials are found, they are well on their way to learning to read water. One way to begin the search for good steelhead-holding water is to exclude those areas that are not suitable to a steelhead's needs.

Charts One and Two on page 44 graphically display the likelihood that steelhead will be present in the various water depths and current speeds we commonly encounter. Remember, these are only general rules that have many exceptions.

A steelhead's main concern is security, they usually seek water that hides them from their enemies. Water speed, water clarity and water depth all play a role in providing cover for a steelhead.

As Chart One shows, the vast majority of steelhead are found in water between three and ten feet deep. You can usually pass by water outside these parameters, thus avoiding areas with a low probability of holding fish. Chart Two shows that most holding steelhead are in water flowing at a rate between three and six knots. Three knots equates to a brisk walk, six knots is equivalent to a fast jog. If you begin your search for steelhead by eliminating very shallow water, very deep water, very slow water and very fast water you have eliminated a large percentage of the river that seldom holds fish.

There are obvious exceptions to these rules. For example, many small rivers have almost no water deeper than three feet. Yet, even here most fish are found in the pockets that offer a good combination of depth and current speed. The combination of water depth, current speed, and, to a lesser extent, oxygen levels dictate the likelihood that a steelhead will be present in an area. Normally you will not find a steelhead holding in water less than three feet deep. The exception being when a rapid current flow provides enough chop and bubbles to hide the fish. These rapid runs also provide added oxygen needed by low water summer fish. Conversely, you seldom find steelhead in dead water with a current flow of less than one knot. The exception being when water depth of eight feet or more obscures the fish from your view. Steelhead often stack in such deep pools in extremely cold weather.

A steelhead's second concern relates to feeding. Some argue that steelhead do not eat after returning to the river as adults. This is simply not true. Anyone who has seen a summer steelhead take a dry fly or a winter fish swallow an egg cluster knows that adult steelhead do feed, sometimes aggressively. Steelhead may feed less aggressively in rivers than they did in the ocean but that is due, at least in part, to the relative lack of food in the river.

On the Stamp River in the winter of 1990 I saw a small hen steelhead take a variety of baits and lures in a fifteen minute period. We had been fishing a seam where the fast, deep water at the outside of a bend met the slower water at the inside of the bend. As our floats trotted down the seam, time and again we would see a strike but just couldn't seem to get a solid hookup. We began by using spawn sacks, switched to sand shrimp and switched again to pink rubber worms. Finally, my float went down and I set the hook on a small chrome-bright fish. After a quick battle we netted it, as it lay flopping on the bottom of our boat the hen spit out two spawn sacks and two sand shrimp. In addition it had struck at my rubber worm which proved to be its downfall. This was a winter fish that was feeding aggressively.

In response to feeding instincts, steelhead often hold in water where fast and slow currents slide together. Serious anglers have long known that these seams, or creases, as the English call them, are superlative holding water. Seams are caused by a variety of river conditions including points jutting into the river, shallow flats dropping suddenly into deeper slots, river bends, rocks, bridge abutments, snags, and other obstructions that significantly change the current flow. Seams are sometimes marked by foam lines, and are usually readily apparent by the distinct line where slick water abuts the choppy riffled water.

Steelhead love to hold at the edge of a seam, hiding from their enemies and feeding on the limited supply of food available in their riparian habitat. In high water steelhead are usually found on the slow side of seams where they can avoid strong currents and find cleaner water. Low water steelhead lie on the fast side of the seam where oxygen levels are higher and the rippled surface provides cover.

Working seams with a float is child's play. If the seam is caused by an in-stream obstruction such as a bridge abutment, boulder or snag, simply cast a bit upstream of the obstruction and work your float down the entire

Fish-holding seams usually are found in sharp river bends. Usually the seam will be in three to six foot deep water where the slower current on the inside of the bend meets the rapid water near the outside bend. A secondary seam may form near the bank on the outside of the bend. Note the holding water behind the boulders.

Even long straight runs produce fish-holding seams. Look for slick water that abuts fast choppy water. These seams are usually nearer the edges of the run than the center.

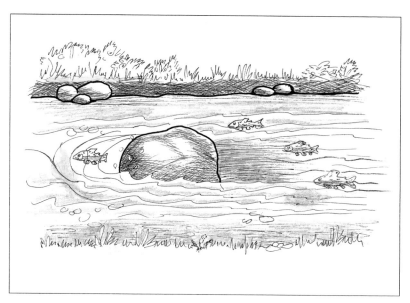

This is classic holding water. If the boulder shows above water, this lie is easy to spot. Many times excellent seams form behind boulders that do not protrude above the surface. These boulders are marked by a disturbance in the surface and the slick that builds behind the boulder.

Instream obstructions almost always cause back-eddies on both sides. The back-eddy in front of an obstruction will not be large enough to hold fish unless the obstruction is quite large. Be sure to work your float in front of and behind obstructions. Cast above the obstruction and let the current sweep it toward the center of the obstruction. Natural hydraulics will push your float around the obstruction. If there is a large back-eddy in front of the obstruction, your float will hold there and swirl around. If the float will not hold in front of the obstruction, the back-eddy is too small to hold fish.

length of the seam. Work the seams on both sides of mid-stream obstructions, then work the area directly in front of and behind the obstruction. There will be a back-eddy on both sides of obstructions, often steelhead hold just behind rock and other obstructions where the back-eddy begins to weaken.

Seams caused by river contours such as curves, drop-offs and points are also easy work. If possible, position yourself above the head of the seam and drift your float down the length of the seam. On the fast side of the seam, let your float drift at the speed of the surface current for two or three drifts, then try a few drifts holding back to slow the lure to a speed near that of the bottom current. On the slow side of the seam let your float dance along at the whim of the current.

Seams are not a constant in a river. In times of extreme high water seams may be found within a few feet of the bank where shoreside bushes and stream contours slow the rushing water. A bait or bright lure worked slowly close to shore will yield fish in a river many would consider unfishable. Even experienced steelheaders overlook these prime seams because

A steelheader works a classic seam on the Gold River. A float allows you to work the seam for as far as you can see.

they are used to looking for fish in the middle of the river. Conversely, in very low water the fish may move from their usual haunts to find shelter in pockets as small as a bathtub. But remember, even these small pockets will invariably be marked by a seam on one side or on both sides.

Comfort is the last of the steelhead's primary needs, but it is an important factor in deciding where they hold. To illustrate how steelhead use current breaks for comfort, Ed Larm, manufacturer of Mr. Ed floats, uses the analogy of a man crossing a field in a wind storm. The man soon discovers that trees and buildings provide respite from the wind. A smart man will move from one windbreak to another as he crosses the field. It's much the same with steelhead working their way upriver. They duck behind rocks, snags or other obstructions to rest before continuing upstream. Savvy steelheaders look for these steelhead rest stops.

In instances of extreme water temperature, flood conditions or drought, comfort considerations force steelhead to move to lies they would not use in normal conditions. If river flows diminish to the point that the steelhead's oxygen needs are not fully met, the fish move to white water riffles and cascades, where oxygen is more abundant. They do this even if these areas do not provide the optimum degree of safety. Conversely, when rivers near flood stage, steelhead move to the edges, sometimes literally into the bushes, where they find cleaner water and the comfort of a slower current.

As water temperatures rise above the steelhead's comfort range they seek pools near the mouth of tributaries and lie near the bottom in the cool water found there. In extremely cold water, steelhead tend to hold near the bottom in deep slow pools. Here they find the security of deep water and expend little effort as they become almost dormant in the still water.

When you hook a steelhead, try to remember two things: First, remember the exact spot you found the fish. On another day, if river conditions are similar, there is a strong chance another steelhead will be in that lie. Second, note the attributes of the spot in which you found your fish. How deep was the run? Was there any structure in the lie that provided a current break? Was the surface choppy, slick, white with bubbles? How fast was the current? If you note these characteristics of a known steelhead lie you will likely notice other areas with similar attributes. Now you know what some of the seats in the theater are like.

There is a good deal more to reading water than the few simple paragraphs above. Entire books have been written on the topic, and even then the authors could not cover all the variables of water temperature, run timing, river height, water clarity, seasonality and a dozen other factors that keep our sport unpredictable and exciting. Reading water is a skill that you will never perfect, but constant observation improves your stream literacy.

Light Line Float Fishing

Steelheaders in the Great Lakes region often fish with lines in the two to four pound test range. In British Columbia and the northwest U.S., most steelheaders consider ten pound test to be light line. Everywhere steelhead thrive, savvy anglers know that light lines often mean more hookups. This is especially true in rivers with slow currents and clear water. Under these conditions, steelhead have the luxury of lots of time and good visibility to thoroughly inspect your offering. If anything looks out of place or the presentation isn't completely natural, steelhead will refuse your lure. This is no place for heavy lines and big hooks.

Float fishing is the ideal approach to light line steelheading. Long rods, center-pin reels, and delicate floats allow a natural presentation that will draw strikes. This tackle provides the strength and sensitivity to hook and land big fish with lines scarcely stronger than spider web.

Success in light line steelheading requires that the rod, line, reel, floats, weights and lures all be selected with light tackle angling in mind. The rod is undoubtedly the most important part of your arsenal. It must have the sensitivity to cushion rapid bursts by steelhead that might weigh as much as five times the breaking strength of your line, yet must have enough backbone to control such a fish. Most light liners choose rods between ten and sixteen feet in length, with the length increasing as line strength decreases. Good rods have a stiff butt section, a softer middle and a very soft tip.

The best reels for light line steelheading are spinning reels or center-pin reels, both of which cast very light

Light lines can account for big fish. Here Nick Amato poses with a sixteen-pound winter steelhead he hooked and landed on eight pound mainline and six pound test leader.

Look at the arc in that rod. Light line steelheading demands long, limber rods that can cushion the shock of a rampaging steelhead.

weight lures. Great Lakes steelheaders prefer center-pin reels for short to medium distance casts and spinning reels where longer casts are necessary. Center-pin reels are cast by stripping off several yards of line with the free hand then flipping the rod in a motion much like that used with a spinning reel. Line is retrieved simply by batting the reel with the free hand. Reel handles are seldom used except when playing a fish.

Because you will be using light lures and small baits, your float needs to be small and sensitive. Long, thin balsa floats are ideal for light line steelheading. Those using dink floats should select the smallest size available, even then you may need to cut off excess material until the float sits low in the water with only a few small shot and your light lure.

Lines of four to six pound test are used for main line. Soft pliable lines work best on both center-pin and spinning reels. Leaders are the other important part of the light liner's arsenal. Light liners go with short, heavy leaders if water is colored—perhaps as heavy as five pound test and as short as eighteen inches. As water currents slow and clarity increases, leaders get longer and lighter. In extreme conditions, leaders of two pound test, eight feet in length may be used.

The purpose of long light leaders is obvious. Or is it? Admittedly, the light lines are harder to see which is an advantage. Perhaps as important is the natural presentation that comes from long, limber leaders. A six foot, two pound test leader rigged with no weight beneath the connecting swivel will allow the lure to swim in a very natural manner. This presentation cannot be matched by short heavy leaders.

Weights used in light lining are special too. With the small floats and tiny lures commonly used, weights must also be small. A variety of split shot sizes are necessary to properly weight the float under varied water conditions. Most light line anglers carry a selection of split shot in segmented containers so they always have the proper size handy.

Here Nick Amato puts the pressure on a light line steelhead. Fish should be played as quickly as possible to avoid undue stress.

Finally, we come to the end of the line—the hook or lure. Most light liners use baits as they lend themselves so well to the natural presentation achieved with floats and light lines. However, artificial flies, Jensen Eggs, and other diminutive lures are also fished with light lines. Hook sizes range from ten to fourteen.

The hold back method of float fishing is more common with light line steelheaders than with others. To achieve the desired natural presentation when holding back with their floats, light liners often set their floats so the distance from the float to the last swivel is roughly equal to the depth of the run they are working.

Weights are arranged with the heaviest near the float. The weights nearest the swivel are very small and unobtrusive. No weights are attached to the long leaders. This weighing arrangement allows the line to curve in a gentle arc from the float to the swivel. The leader precedes the line with the bait fluttering alluringly just above the bottom.

When a strike comes, the hookset must be quick but not overly aggressive. Many fish are broken off with an assertive strike. With very light lines, you may have to simply lift the rod until you feel tension, then set the hook with only a gentle upward swing of the rod tip.

Fighting the fish with light lines is also a matter of finesse versus strength. When a hot fish runs downriver, you must also run downriver. If you let the fish have its head, i.e. don't apply much pressure, it will often turn and come back to its lie. If you keep the pressure on, it may well spool you. Rods designed for two to six pound test line bend almost double without breaking. Once the fish is partially tired you need to start applying all the pressure the rod can stand. A long handled net will shorten the battle dramatically, avoiding the stand off that otherwise might occur when the fish is tired but not quite tired enough to beach.

Remember that steelhead can be terminally stressed by excessively long battles. If you intend to release your fish, bring it to hand as quickly as possible. Once you have the fish in control either in the net or at your feet, the easiest way to release it is to grasp the leader near the hook and break the line with a quick snap. The hook will soon rub off, or rust away.

Today few steelheaders outside the Great Lakes region routinely fish with lines lighter than six pound test. As the effectiveness of this technique becomes better known, the practice will undoubtedly spread throughout the range of steelhead and their pursuers.

Advanced Techniques

The techniques described thus far will serve in most situations you might encounter. Yet, there are a few tricks that the top rods have developed which will allow you to effectively fish areas that are unapproachable with traditional float fishing methods. It always seems the water that lies just out of reach looks the most promising. Perhaps these tricks will allow you to fish a few more of these tantalizing places.

Pop-Up Floats

On occasion we find a long flat that looks as though the entire length may hold fish. Near the end of the run a deep pool forms. If we can boat or walk to the tail of the run, we can fish it and the pool beneath, but sometimes this is not possible. Our only choice for fishing the far end of such a run is to drift our float on a very long drift. There are three problems with this; it is very difficult to see a strike when the float is more than one hundred feet away; there are often shallow stretches between us and the deeper pool we want to fish; hook-sets are difficult when we are more than one hundred feet from our float. The pop-up float resolves two of these three problems.

Yvonne Munson poses in a thoroughly Canadian steelheading scene. Note the center-pin reel, and the Gooey Bob hanging from this wild steelhead's mouth.

To rig a pop-up float, remove most or all weight from your float and attach a small bait or light weight lure. This will cause your float to lay over on its side. Now free spool and work the float toward the water you want to fish. As the float approaches shallows, hold back until the float points upstream and your lure trails out behind. This will allow you to ease past the shallows. As the float approaches the water you want to fish, resume free spooling letting your lure and float drift through the holding water naturally.

When a strike comes, the float will pop up, then slip underwater. Even from several hundred feet upstream, you should have no trouble seeing the float flip over then slip under. It will be difficult to get a solid hookset from extreme distances. Your best chance is to quickly dip your rod tip to the water, reel in all the slack and come back high and hard with your rod. Do your best to sweep your rod tip as far up and back as possible.

The pop-up float will give you access to waters you might have passed over but at a price of more missed strikes. Still, it's better to have struck and missed than never to have struck at all.

Slip Floats

For many steelheaders, slip floats are an every day part of their arsenal. However, the majority of steelheaders who use floats are not familiar with slip floats and many more steelheaders have no experience with floats of any type. To them the slip float represents a step beyond their present experience.

Slip floats do as the name implies. They slip on the line to a predetermined stopping point, allowing you to fish any depth you desire. When you find yourself fishing water greater than ten feet deep, you want to switch to a slip float.

Most of the floats currently marketed can be used as slip floats. Any float with a central hollow core from top to bottom will serve. To rig the slip float, you need only two items in addition to the usual float tackle—a bead and a stopper.

To rig your slip float you must first affix a stopper to your line. Then thread a small bead on your line. Next thread the line through the hollow tube of your float and attach a swivel in the usual manner. For a stopper most anglers use a nail knot tied with brightly colored Dacron fly line backing. Several manufacturers market nail knot stoppers, these are usually nothing more than a hollow tube upon which one to six nail knots are tied. To use these slip your main line through the hollow tube then slip a nail knot from the tube onto your line. Now snug the nail knot very tight and trim the loose ends, leaving about an inch of line extending from each end of the knot. This knot will slip easily on a wetted line and is very visible.

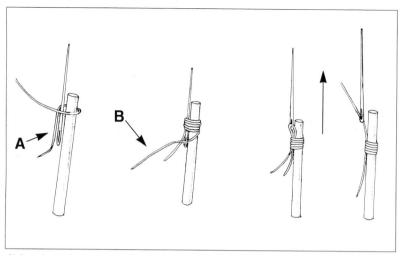

1) Lay doubled wire or crochet needle on tube; 2) Hold at arrow (A); 3) Begin wraps; 4) Make five wraps and tuck wrapping end (B) through eye of needle or doubled wire. 5) Pull needle or doubled wire to pull wrapping end through (underneath) wraps; 6) Tighten and clip ends leaving 1 1/4" ends.

Now you are ready to fish a slip float. All you need do is estimate the depth of the water you wish to fish and slip the bobber stop an appropriate distance up your main line. (Nail knots slip much more easily on a wet line). Reel until you have a foot or so of line from the float to your rod tip and make your cast.

Once the float lands, the main line will slip through the float and bead until the bead makes contact with the stopper. If you find that your float has settled low in the water with just a bit of the top showing, you know you

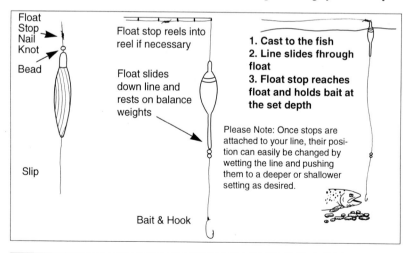

Float Stop

Nail Knot

Bead

Slip

Float stop reels into reel if necessary

Float slides down line and rests on balance weights

Bait & Hook

1. Cast to the fish
2. Line slides fhrough float
3. Float stop reaches float and holds bait at the set depth

Please Note: Once stops are attached to your line, their position can easily be changed by wetting the line and pushing them to a deeper or shallower setting as desired.

have weighted your float well and that the lure is suspended above the bottom. If your float rides unnaturally high or lays on its side, you can be sure the bobber stop was placed too high and your lure is resting on the bottom. As you retrieve line, the float stop will pass easily through the rod guides. There may be a slight twitch as the stop slips over the guides, but nothing more. Likewise the stop should present no problem in casting. (If you leave about an inch of line extending from each end of the nail knot it will slide through the guides more easily than if it is trimmed short.)

Rather than pass by deep runs, consider slip floats. Slip floats give you access to some quality waters that can be fished well no other way.

Fishing With a Center-Pin Reel

In British Columbia, home of float fishing for steelhead, most of the serious steelheaders use a center-pin or single action reel. The same is true in much of the Midwest steelheading country. These reels look a bit like a fly reel and operate much the same. There are no gears to speed your rate of retrieve and the drag is either nonexistent or quite light.

Almost all center-pin reels are of the highest quality construction; most feature smooth-as-silk bearings that let the spool revolve almost effortlessly. Most are built from a single block of aluminum and most are quite expensive. These reels are highly prized by their owners and for good reason.

A center-pin reel in the hands of an experienced steelheader will cast a float and lure beautifully. In addition, few other reels free spool as effortlessly. When you are trying to walk your float down a seam on the far side of the river, the center-pin is the perfect reel for the job. The small spools and less-than-perfect bearings of many bait casting reels create drag as the spool turns. This drag is telegraphed to your float and eventually pulls the float away from the drift you were working. A good center-pin reel will keep your float in the strike zone longer.

Lack of a mechanical drag system increases the challenge of fighting a steelhead. Drag can be applied in one of two ways, either with the bottom edge of the palm of your casting hand or with the palm of the other hand. Some anglers hold the rod with their left hand just above the reel's rim. To free spool, they simply move their palm away from the spool. To increase drag, they add pressure with their palm. This will serve for controlling casts and for holding back the float, but when a big steelhead charges off downstream, most anglers use the palm of their right hand under the spool for added braking.

The marvelous smoothness of the center-pin is a mixed blessing. These reels cast forever, but they also throw a major league bird's nest. The only backlash prevention device these reels feature is an educated palm. Some would-be center-pin fishers have gone back to their bait casting reels in frus-

tration after spending the day picking out backlashes and finding their longest cast to be something short of fifty feet. My first three casts with a center-pin all failed to make it to the water!

Casting the center-pin reel is as easy as riding a bicycle, i.e impossible until you get the hang of it, ridiculously easy after that. Those who have never cast a bait casting reel may find it easier to master the center-pin reel than those who have developed a feel for the bait caster. I know all my years with a bait casting reel contributed to the difficulty I had in learning to handle a center-pin. They are completely different reels and the dynamics of casting them are quite different.

The photo above demonstrates the proper mechanics for long casts with heavy weights or lures.

The most important difference between casting with a center-pin and a level wind is the release point. With the level wind, the rod is brought back fully loaded and has begun the forward cast before the spool is released. With a center-pin the spool must begin revolving before the back cast is complete. An instant before you start to bring the rod forward, you must release the spool or give it a spin to allow the spool to begin freely rotating before you begin your forward cast. This allows the spool to come up to speed gradually. If you try casting the center-pin reel without releasing the spool until after the rod begins its forward motion, you will find yourself with a very short cast, a major bird's nest, or both.

If you are working water within thirty feet of your casting position, simply strip a few feet of line from the reel and flip the lure twenty to thirty feet. Such short casts when coupled with rods in the twelve foot range let you fish the majority of many small streams.

If you are using small lures and light weights, you may want to try casting the center-pin as if it were a spinning reel. To do this, you need to hold the spool with the thumb of your casting hand. Using the index finger of

Top steelheaders have an arsenal of tricks in their bag. This twenty plus pound Thompson River steelhead was holding in a deep run. The best way to fish such deep runs is with a slip float.

your other hand grasp the line approximately a foot above the point where the line leaves the spool. Now pull the line back until it's approximately a foot above and directly in line with the center of the reel. Begin your cast with the spool firmly held by your thumb and the line lifted above the center of the reel with the index finger of the opposite hand.

You have now effectively converted your center-pin to a spinning reel. To cast you must keep the spool stationary. When you cast with the same motion as you would with a spinning reel, the line will flow off the spool and over the index finger, much like it would with a spinning reel.

Bottom Bouncing With a Float

Many expert float fishers rig their floats to allow their weights—usually slinkys—to continuously drag bottom. Other experienced float fishers feel this practice is a perversion that negates most of the benefits of traditional float fishing.

Proponents of the bottom bouncing float system argue that this technique gives them the best of both worlds. By keeping in contact with the bottom, they are certain their lure is deep enough, and the drag of bottom bouncing slows their lure allowing the fish more time to see and strike. The float still provides the benefits of fewer hang-ups, a visual strike indicator and precise placement of the lure.

Others argue that dragging the bottom results in an unnatural presentation, increases the number of hang-ups and reduces the float's value as a strike indicator because the frequent bottom bouncing drags the float under so often it is difficult to tell a strike from snagging the bottom. I have seen the bottom bouncing float technique perform quite well and on many occasions it appears to outfish traditional float fishing techniques. Of the five best steelheaders I know, two use the technique regularly, one tries it occasionally and two seldom do. I believe the bottom bouncing technique can be of value in fast water. It would be a definite detriment in very slow or still water. You can choose for yourself, but to make a well informed choice you should give it a try.

Float Fishing with Buoyant Lures

Many steelhead lures are buoyant. Lures such as Cheaters, Corkies and Spin and Glows all work well. They all share the common attributes of a hollow center tube, through which the leader is passed, and buoyancy. When these lures are rigged in the usual manner and fished beneath a float, two problems can arise—the lure tends to float too high and it may slip up the leader and away from the bait or yarn.

To keep buoyant lures in the steelhead's strike zone, a little more weight must be added to the equation. Weight the float in your usual manner, then add two tiny split shot approximately six inches above the buoyant lure. The secondary set of weights will hold your lure in the strike zone and will not spook the fish.

Buoyant lures fish very well with the bottom bouncing technique mentioned earlier. When your weight ticks bottom, the lure will be forced in to the strike zone. This also assures that lures designed to rotate have sufficient current passing over them to do their job.

As the float and lure work downstream, hold back to let the buoyant lure precede the main line. The first thing the steelhead sees is your lure.

A second problem with buoyant lures is that they tend to creep up the leader. Sometimes the current pushes the lure back to your hook, but often it remains well above the hook causing a wasted cast and often a tangle. This is easily resolved with two small beads and the float fisher's constant companion—the toothpick.

When rigging with a buoyant lure, first slip a small bead down to the hook, then slip the buoyant lure down to the bead and follow it with another small bead. Hold the upper bead approximately one half inch above the buoyant lure and peg it in place with a toothpick. Break off the excess toothpick and you are ready to fish. The upper bead will keep the lure from slipping up the leader and the lower one acts as a bearing, allowing the lure to spin freely as intended.

Float Fishing With Spinners

Steelhead love spinners. Experienced steelheaders hate to leave good holding water without tossing a spinner a few times. They know steelhead often ignore prime baits and all other lures only to pounce on a spinner. Float fishers can work spinners as well or better than bottom bouncers if they follow a few simple tips.

To work correctly, a spinner must have water flowing against the blade. To accomplish this, float anglers need to be certain they are upstream from the suspected lie and must hold back the float as it drifts downstream. That's really all there is to it.

Many B.C. float fishers prefer Colorado spinners over other varieties because they spin with very little water pressure across the blade. This is ideal for the presentation style of float fishers. Any traditional steelhead spinner will work beneath the float as long as you can hold back the float enough to get the blade spinning.

Conclusion

I hope *Float Fishing for Steelhead* has given you all you expected. My intention in writing this book was to increase your pleasure in our mutual sport. I sincerely hope that whatever added knowledge this book may have provided will not be used to the detriment of our partners in this sport—the steelhead.

Wild steelhead are in a state of decline throughout much of their range. There are plenty of targets at which we sportsmen can point our fingers. Greed is the root cause of the steelhead's decline. Greed of the timber companies that refuse to leave adequate buffers along stream banks, greed of net fishermen who indiscriminately slaughter steelhead as an incidental bycatch, greed of ranchers who refuse to fence livestock out of the streams, and, perhaps worst of all, greed of "sportsmen" who kill wild steelhead so they can show off to their friends or put a steelhead in the smoker.

When you consider the tremendous obstacles the wild steelhead overcame to arrive back at its birth stream, it seems an abomination to kill them. Returning steelhead have survived two to three years in the stream where other fish, birds, mammals, drought, flood, pollution and disease did their best to do them in. Less than 4 percent made it to the ocean where another series of obstacles thinned their ranks. Upon return to their natal streams these noble survivors face concentrations of marine mammals, pollution, nets and a phalanx of sports anglers all eager to terminate their journey as success is almost in sight. After the steelhead succeeds in spawning, it will run the gauntlet back to the ocean and return to spawn again, if the Gods be willing.

It is these genetically superior wild steelhead we must protect at all costs. There is little we can do about corporate greed, but we can and should do all we can to act ethically as we pursue our sport. In several states and provinces wild steelhead are protected by regulation. This is as it should be. In unenlightened states and provinces where you have the choice to kill or release wild steelhead, your ethics must be stronger than the laws passed by legislators who gave in to the greed of special interest groups.

Hatchery-reared steelhead were planted to be harvested. I feel no compunction in harvesting these domesticated steelhead. In British Columbia where catch and release is a firmly ingrained ethic, steelheaders voluntarily release most hatchery fish. Where we have rivers with both hatchery and wild steelhead, some anglers believe it is their duty to kill any hatchery fish caught to keep it from interbreeding with wild fish. Whether or not we choose to release a hatchery-reared steelhead is and should be a matter of personal preference.

When we hold a wild steelhead in our hands, we hold an ever rarer treasure. There can be no excuse for purposely destroying such a treasure. Those who doubt that man can, and would if given the chance, force wild steelhead into extinction, should remember the passenger pigeon, the buffalo, and all the others forever gone. Enjoy our wild steelhead when you can and protect them always.

Where to Find Tackle

Rods

G. Loomis, P.O. Box U, Woodland, WA 98674
The world leader in steelhead float rods as well as also offering a large selection of blanks.

Lindy-Little Joe, Inc., Box C, Brainerd, MN 56401
Features a top quality float rod as well as a wide selection of floats and terminal gear.

Lamiglas, 1359 Downriver Drive, Woodland, WA 98674
Top quality and toughness are the trademark of Lamiglas. This long time steelhead rod manufacturer has just introduced a line of float rods.

Reels

Abu-Garcia, 21 Law Drive, Airfield, NJ 07004
Durable Dependable level wind bait casting reels. Proven quality over several generations.

Shimano American Corp., POB 19615, Irvine, CA 92718
Precision level wind reels.

Floats

Lindy-Little Joe, Inc., Boc C, Brainerd, MN 56401
Lindy carries a complete line of Thill balsa floats as well as a fine selection of terminal gear.

Mr. Eds Floats, 4001 S.E. Crown Rd. Camas, WA 98607
Ed has a full line of dink floats in every size and color. A unique design holds the float securely while allowing rapid adjustments.

B & D Tackle, 2245 Austin Ave., Coquitlam, B.C. Canada V3K 3R9
B & D Manufactures a full line of balsa floats with a solid plastic center tube which allows them to be used as slip floats or quickly adjustable fixed floats.

Class Tackle, (Balsa Floats) 5719 Corporation Circle, Unit 1, Fort Meyers, FL 33905, 800-869-9941.

Float Fishing Specialist, (Distance Casters and Others) 5604 Wood Valley Drive, Haslett, MI 48840, (517) 339-8971.